HISTORICAL SKETCH

OF

MOUNT HOLYOKE SEMINARY.

FOUNDED AT SOUTH HADLEY, MASS., IN 1837.

Prepared in compliance with an invitation from the Commissioner of Education, representing the Department of the Interior in matters relating to the National Centennial of 1876.

BY MARY O. NUTTING, LIBRARIAN.

WASHINGTON:
GOVERNMENT PRINTING OFFICE.
1876.

PREFATORY NOTE.

The following summary of the history of Mount Holyoke Seminary is sent out as a specimen of the work in course of preparation for the Centennial of 1876, and as covering the leading points of inquiry embraced in a series of circulars issued from the Bureau of Education to institutions authorized by law to confer degrees, with the view of collecting materials for a general report upon superior education for that occasion.

There are many seminaries of great merit which do not strictly come within this definition, still it is desirable that the data concerning them should be fully procured, and a circular will soon be issued from the Bureau of Education, recommending that all educational institutions of the academic class, including the graded schools of cities and villages, improve the occasion of the centennial year by preparing for their annual catalogue, or report for 1876, histories of their own institutions substantially upon the plan of this pamphlet, and illustrated so far as may be practicable.

To give the greatest possible value to this local publication, a general interchange is recommended, the details of which are set forth in the circular above referred to, and which will be sent to each institution receiving this pamphlet.

Such institutions as intend to co-operate in this measure are requested to notify the undersigned as soon as practicable. A general summary of the whole series embraced in the interchange will be made as fully as the data allow and sent to each institution.

FRANKLIN B. HOUGH.

BUREAU OF EDUCATION,
Washington, D. C., January 27, 1876.

MOUNT HOLYOKE FEMALE SEMINARY.

LOCATION AND BUILDINGS.

This institution is situated in the village of South Hadley, Hampshire County, Massachusetts. It is nearly two miles east of the Connecticut River, and thirteen miles north of Springfield. Northampton lies five miles to the northwest, Amherst ten miles north. Mount Holyoke, from which the institution derives its name, is four miles north of the village. The scenery of the region is noted for its quiet and varied beauty. The broad, tranquil river, after lingering a little in the lovely Northampton meadows, sweeps southward past Mount Holyoke on the left, and then for miles along the base of Mount Tom on the right. To the eastward the valley here spreads into broad and fertile fields, dotted with graceful elms. Everywhere one finds something in the landscape to admire. The village is a quiet and attractive one, which had the preference over other places in the region whose advantages had caused them to be proposed as the seat of the institution.

The seminary stands on the east side of the main street, some forty rods south of the hotel and the church. Its buildings are but a little withdrawn from the well-shaded highway, the grounds lying chiefly in the rear, and sloping at length to the edge of a picturesque stream. This stream, being no less industrious than picturesque, finds occasion to spread into a pretty little pond, just as it reaches the seminary grounds, and again, just below them, into a larger one, where much rowing and skating are done by the young ladies.

The brook is crossed by a rustic foot-bridge, and beyond rises a well-rounded and lofty hill which commands charming views of the neighboring country.

The grounds at present comprise about fifteen acres, some five or six acres having been purchased within a few years. The frontage on the street is something over thirty rods, the depth nearly seventy, to the stream, which originally formed the eastern boundary. In addition to this, there is a field containing one or two acres on the opposite side of the brook. The original lot is bordered by a fine belt of trees planted twenty-five or thirty years ago, and there are other trees along the banks of the stream that are much older. Although little has yet been attempted in the way of ornamentation, nature has almost performed the part of a landscape-gardener; and though she may have left something to wish for, she has certainly bestowed much to admire.

The various buildings have been erected or enlarged from time to time, as required by the development of the institution. The main edifice, which fronts west, is 166 by 50 feet, and four stories high. At each end is a wing, 122 by 40, standing at right angles to the main building. The eastern extremities of the two wings are connected by the gymnasium, thus forming a quadrangle. The library is a fire-proof structure, 48 by 33, with an arched recess 12 by 6 on each side. It was erected six years since, and stands directly north of the main edifice, to which it is joined by a corridor 45 by 11 feet. A new building, commenced in 1875, and designed for laboratory, museums, and art-gallery, stands apart from the others, a little distance to the northeast. It is 66 by 63 feet, with a wing 40 by 24 feet. It is of brick with stone finishings, like those previously mentioned, but is more modern in its style. The present observatory is scarcely more than a shelter for a good refracting telescope, with an object-glass six inches in diameter. The instrument was presented by Rev. Mr. Dickinson, of Durham, Middlesex County, Connecticut, some twenty years ago. Of late the surrounding trees have encroached upon its field of observation to an inconvenient extent, and a new building will be erected in a more favorable spot as soon as funds shall be at command.

The buildings now in use, aside from the library, are valued at about two hundred thousand dollars. The library, with its contents, is worth probably not less than thirty-five thousand, and the building for science and art will cost sixty thousand. The value of the various cabinets, herbarium, &c., cannot at present be definitely stated, as many of the specimens cannot even be accessible to the pupils, for want of room to arrange them, until the new building shall be finished.

BENEFACTIONS.

The institution has no endowment, and has received few large donations from any source. Once only it has been aided by the State. In 1867, a debt of twenty-seven thousand dollars having been incurred, partly in building the gymnasium and extending the south wing and partly in purchasing more land, a grant of forty thousand dollars was solicited and obtained. The gift of ten thousand dollars for books, from Mrs. H. F. Durant, has been mentioned in the sketch of the library. The late Miss Phebe Hazeltine, of Boscawen, N. H., bequeathed fifteen thousand dollars to establish a fund for the assistance of deserving pupils. Certain smaller sums given for the same object by other donors, added to this, make in all about twenty thousand. The annual income from this fund furnishes assistance, to some extent, to a number of young ladies who could not otherwise have the advantages of a superior education. The sum of three thousand six hundred dollars was bequeathed to the institution a few years since by the late Mrs. Julia M. Tolman, once associate principal, to begin a fund whose income might be used for the benefit of teachers.

Of the subscriptions for the building now in progress, the largest thus far is one of seven thousand five hundred dollars from A. L. Williston, esq., of Northampton, the present treasurer of the Seminary. A few other individuals have given sums ranging from five hundred dollars to two thousand dollars; but in general, as in the case of the first building, the donations have been numerous rather than of large amount.

ORIGIN AND EARLY HISTORY.

Mary Lyon, the founder of Mount Holyoke Seminary, was born in Buckland, Franklin County, Massachusetts, on the twenty-eighth of February, 1797. She was endowed with a superior intellect, as well as extraordinary physical vigor.* To these was added a religious character of corresponding depth and power, which fitted her to become one of the world's benefactors. Her education was obtained by no small effort and self-denial, which, however, were made light by her intense desire for knowledge. From 1824 to 1834 she was associated with the eminent and accomplished Miss Grant† in conducting at first the Adams Female Academy,

* The Rev. Dr. Todd, in a private letter dated in March, 1849, remarks as follows:

"Miss Lyon is suddenly cut off from a life of great usefulness; but God does not need any one instrument with which to carry on his plans. She was an extraordinary woman, having more physical, intellectual, and moral strength united in her than I ever saw in any other woman."

† Afterwards the wife of the Hon. William B. Banister, of Newburyport. Mrs. B. died in December, 1874, having retained to the age of fourscore the bright intellect, the rare conversational powers, and the warm Christian benevolence characteristic of her earlier years.

at Derry, N. H., and afterward the Female Seminary at Ipswich, in the eastern part of Massachusetts. While thus engaged she began to long for the establishment of a permanent institution for the education of young women, whose expenses should be so moderate as not to debar those of limited means, and whose advantages so great that the wealthy could find none superior elsewhere. The problem was not easy to solve. Hitherto it had been generally supposed that girls needed but little education, and that chiefly ornamental. The schools which private individuals, here and there, had found it convenient to carry on, sufficed to give a smattering of certain accomplishments to the daughters of affluence, and there were district schools for the rest. What more could be desired? Why should colleges be established, with faculties, buildings, libraries, cabinets, and apparatus, merely to educate girls?

For a long time the public could not be awakened to the importance of the subject. The rich were even more indifferent than the middle classes. But none the less did Miss Lyon ponder the needs, the duties, the possibilities of woman, till the great enterprise had absorbed her whole soul. "Had I a thousand lives," she wrote, "I could sacrifice them all in suffering and hardship for its sake Did I possess the greatest fortune, I could readily relinquish it all, and become poor, and more than poor, if its prosperity should demand it." It was not merely as a grand and ennobling possession that she coveted education for her sex. Culture was to be not so much the end as the means. The pupils were to be trained to help themselves mainly for the sake of helping others. They were to seek knowledge not simply to enjoy it, but rather that they might become the stronger to uplift, the wiser to guide, those who needed their aid. After years of patient thought, prayer, and effort, the way was opened. Leaving Ipswich in 1834, Miss Lyon devoted herself to the task of establishing the new institution. Little by little, funds were collected for the first building. In the record of those gifts, one may discover many a donation of half a dollar. But the half dollars from those slender purses were offered by cordial hands, and a blessing was on them. The act of incorporation passed the legislature February 10, 1836, and was signed by the governor on the following day. The corner-stone of a four-story brick building 94 by 50 feet was laid on the 3d of October following, and the school was opened on the 8th of November, 1837.

Among the earliest and most active friends of the enterprise should be mentioned Rev. Roswell Hawks, of Cummington, Mass, Hon. Daniel Safford, of Boston, and A. W. Porter, esq., of Monson, Mass. Mr. Hawks was enlisted in the cause as permanent agent as early as 1834. From town to town in Western Massachusetts, and from house to house, he presented its claims, with such clearness, good sense, and patient persistence as to win people who had never before dreamed of doing anything for female education. Always devoted to the interests of the institution, he was president of its board of trustees for many years, and subsequently assisted in establishing the Lake Erie Seminary, at Painesville, Ohio, one of the earliest offshoots from the Holyoke stock.

Mr. Safford, a prosperous business man, who had long been accustomed to devote most of his income to works of benevolence, was another of the first trustees of the seminary. To him and to his excellent wife it was indebted not only for pecuniary aid, but also for counsel, sympathy, and co-operation more precious than gold. They were with Miss Lyon, heart and hand, in the days when public prejudice was yet to be conquered and public confidence to be won.

They shared personally in the anxieties and toils of organizing the seminary family for the first time; they watched the progress of the enterprise as years passed on, ever caring for its interests, praying for its prosperity, and rejoicing in its success. In his last days, Mr. Safford remarked, "No money, time, or effort which I have bestowed on any object affords me more satisfaction in the review than what I have given to Mount Hoyloke Seminary."

Mr. Porter became a trustee in March, 1836. The enterprise had then reached a point where it required a gentleman to superintend the erection of the building. It must be one whose business ability had been tested, whose integrity would inspire public confidence, and who would wish no remuneration. Mr. Porter was the man. For months, leaving his own extensive business in the charge of others, he used to drive every Monday morning from Monson to South Hadley, a distance of twenty miles, and there till Saturday would devote himself to the affairs of the Seminary. From those days almost to the present time, each successive addition or reconstruction has received from him the same faithful, disinterested, judicious care. For many years he was treasurer of the institution, receiving and disbursing its modest income with a fidelity and prudence unsurpassed. His admirable wife, a lady of superior culture and worth, shared fully his almost parental interest in the seminary; and both regarded its teachers and pupils as in some measure supplying the place of the children whom they had lost. In the serene and beautiful evening of his days, Mr. Porter still remains the most valued counselor of the seminary, and the only surviving member of its first board of trustees.

Others of that band are held in most grateful remembrance, but the limits of this article permit the naming of only one or two. Professor Edward Hitchcock, afterward the president of Amherst College, was ever a most devoted and valued friend to Miss Lyon and to Mount Holyoke Seminary. Mr. Avery, of Conway, Mass., also rendered important services to the cause in many ways.*

LIBRARY OF MOUNT HOLYOKE SEMINARY.

In 1857 the library of this Seminary contained about four thousand volumes, mostly of well-selected and valuable books. The late Dr. Kirk and Deacon Safford, of Boston, should be remembered as friends to the library during its early years. The latter took great interest in personally supervising the enlargement and refitting of the room during the summer of 1855, and only a few months before his death.

In 1867, the wife of one of the trustees, (Henry F. Durant, founder of Wellesley College,) proposed to give ten thousand dollars for the purchase of books, provided that a suitable fire-proof library building should be erected within three years. The trustees accordingly proceeded to build, a grant from the State about that time having put it within their power to do so, and in November, 1870, the new edifice was ready.

The building was designed by the late Hammet Billings, of Boston, and cost about eighteen thousand dollars. The interior is handsomely finished in chestnut, with frescoed ceiling, and a spacious bay-window in an arched recess on either side. The book-cases and other furniture are of black walnut, finely carved. The alcoves are arranged so as to form cozy nooks for the readers, who have free access to the shelves at any hour of the day. At present the shelves will

* Those desiring fuller accounts of Miss Lyon and her colaborers are referred to the following works: Life of Mary Lyon, published by the American Tract Society, New York. Recollections of Mary Lyon: American Tract Society of Boston. Daniel Safford: Congregational Publishing Society, Boston. Memorial Volume of Mount Holyoke Seminary: South Hadley, 1862.

accommodate about twelve or fourteen thousand volumes only, but by introducing galleries room could readily be made for several thousand more; and by an addition in the rear the capacity of the building might be increased indefinitely. The present number of books is about nine thousand, not including the valuable library bequeathed to the Seminary by the late Dr. Kirk, which is soon to be received, and will form an important acquisition. Great care has been bestowed upon the selection of the books by Mr. Durant, assisted by eminent librarians, and it is often remarked that few collections of the size are as valuable as this. The greater part of the books are in elegant and durable bindings. As they have been chosen with especial reference to the various courses of study pursued here, teachers and pupils are able to consult a wide range of authorities upon any topic before them. The library is generously supplied with the works of the earlier English poets, dramatists, and chroniclers, as well as with those of modern times. It has also about five hundred volumes in French, German, and Italian, and nearly three hundred in Latin and Greek. Among the latter are Valpy's edition of the Latin classics, in one hundred and forty-one octavo volumes, and Trübner's edition of Latin and Greek classics, in one hundred and twenty-seven volumes. The scientific department contains various costly illustrated works, and there is a good collection of books on art. The department of periodical literature includes full sets of several foreign reviews and magazines. The system of cataloguing is similar to that of the Boston Public Library, having besides the reception catalogue a catalogue upon cards, which are arranged alphabetically according to names of authors. A classified index also is in progress. As yet the library has no permanent fund, but efforts will be made to secure one at no distant day, so that it may have the means of a constant and liberal growth.

PLAN OF EDUCATION AND COURSE OF STUDY.

"The grand features of this institution," wrote Miss Lyon before its opening, "are to be an elevated standard of science, literature, and refinement, and a moderate standard of expense, all to be guided and modified by the spirit of the gospel." She did not propose to provide for the entire school education, but only for the later years of it. As candidates could be fitted elsewhere, it was not considered needful or expedient to open a preparatory department. The course proposed was solid rather than showy. Considerable advancement in study, as well as some maturity of character, was needful in order to pursue it with advantage. Candidates passed examinations in English Grammar, Geography, United States History, Mental and Written Arithmetic, and Watts on the Mind. The regular course, as shown by the earliest catalogues, commenced with such studies as Euclid, Ancient History, Botany, Physiology, and Rhetoric, and went on, through the three years, up to Logic, Mental and Moral Philosophy, and Butler's Analogy. Latin was not then embraced in the curriculum, though it was from the first strongly advised as an optional study, and as early as 1840 about one-fourth of the pupils were voluntarily pursuing it. After 1846, candidates were required to have mastered at least the Latin Grammar and Reader before entering; and some of the Latin classics were thenceforth included in the course.

In looking over the earlier catalogues, one observes, perhaps with a little surprise, that Sullivan's Political Class-Book and Wayland's Political Economy were included in the course. Forty years ago woman's rights were not much talked of, and certainly Miss Lyon had not the ballot-box in view in proposing these studies. She was a far-seeing woman, however, and meant her pupils to be intelligent on great subjects, even outside the field where their personal duties were expected to lie.

In planning the course, Miss Lyon was perfectly aware that there would be many pupils who could pursue it for only a year or two. Want of pecuniary means, the claims of friends at home, engagements to be fulfilled, or other imperative reasons, would often decide the question beforehand beyond appeal. To spend even one year in such a school was to these a great boon; they accepted it thankfully and made much of it. Following the regular course while they remained, they laid a good foundation for whatever they might find opportunity to acquire after leaving. Of late years, a much larger proportion of the young ladies enter intending to complete the course, and actually do so. Candidates are not admitted until they are sixteen years of age, and many are older. The age of the present junior class, at admission, averaged eighteen years and two months. The age at graduation is generally between twenty-one and twenty-two. The whole number of graduates, including the class of 1876, is fifteen hundred and sixty-eight.

Since 1862, the regular course has occupied four years. There are optional courses in French, German, and Greek, which may be pursued in addition to the former, but are not to be substituted for any portion of it. Candidates for admission are examined in English Analysis, Elementary Algebra, Physical Geography, and Harkness's Latin Grammar and Reader, as well as in the preparatory studies previously mentioned.* The regular course at present is as follows:

JUNIOR YEAR.

Nepos or Sallust.
Olney's Algebra.

---

* Excepting Watts on the Mind.

Ancient History, (Willson's University Edition.)
Dalton's Physiology.
Nicholl's Introduction to the Study of the Bible.
Gray's Botany.

JUNIOR MIDDLE YEAR.

Cicero de Senectute.
Loomis's Geometry.
Modern History, (Willson's University Edition.)
Zoölogy.
Hart's Rhetoric.
Andrews's Manual of United States Constitution
Gray's Botany.

SENIOR MIDDLE YEAR.

Virgil.
Loomis's Trigonometry.
Barker's Chemistry.
Atkinson's Ganot's Physics.
Kiddle's Astronomy.
Chadbourne's Natural Theology.
History of English Literature.

SENIOR YEAR.

Cicero de Immortalitate.
Dana's Geology and Mineralogy.
Hickok's Psychology.
Schlegel's History of Literature.
Hickok's Moral Science.
Evidences of Christianity.
Butler's Analogy.

The following are the optional courses already mentioned:

GREEK COURSE.

First year.—Leighton's Greek Lessons—Goodwin's Grammar—Xenophon—Jones's Exercises in Composition.

Second year.—Herodotus and Thucydides—Homer—Jones's Exercises.

Third year.—Hadley's Grammar—Demosthenes—Greek Drama—Boises' Exercises in Composition.

Fourth year.—Plato—Greek Drama—Exercises in Composition.

FRENCH COURSE.

First year.—Keetel's Grammar—Reading.

Second year.—Languellier and Monsanto's French Course—Dictées de l'Hôtel de Ville—Reading: Selections from Mme. de Staël.

Third year.—Cours lexicologique de Style, by M. P. Larousse—Dictées de l'Hôtel de Ville—Reading: Works of Molière, Racine, &c.

Fourth year.—Cours lexicologique de Style—French Compositions—Sainte-Beuve's Portraits des Femmes, and other classical authors—Conversation each year.

GERMAN COURSE.

First year.—Grammar: Exercises and Reading.

Second year.—Grammar continued—Translations—Schiller's Jungfrau von Orleans.

Third year.—Schiller's Thirty Years' War—Gœthe's and Uhland's Minor Poems.

Fourth year.—Vilmar's Geschichte der deutschen Literatur—Reading of classic German authors.

The intellectual labor required amounts to about six hours a day; that is, two recitations of forty-five minutes, and four hours and a half spent in study. As a rule, only two studies are pursued at a time, though one may have, besides, a brief exercise in elocution, penmanship, drawing, or painting; and nearly all take lessons two or three times a week in vocal music and gymnastics. There are but four recitation-days in the week, a fifth being devoted to English composition and general business. Several courses of lectures in the various departments of study are given each year by eminent professors.

Much besides mere intellectual furnishing and drill has always been aimed at by this institution. That would be a very incomplete education which should leave out of sight the habits of self-control, system, punctuality, and general efficiency which are so indispensable to a woman. In the conditions of the large household, there was not a little which favored the cultivation of these traits, and Miss Lyon knew how to turn it to the best account. Among so many it was needful for each to refrain from whatever might disturb or hinder others; and there was occasion for careful planning and prompt performing in order to accomplish one's various duties. Moreover, each perceived that she was only one member of a numerous household, and that something pertaining to its comfort devolved upon her, for which she soon learned to hold herself responsible day by day. For it has ever been a family as truly as a school; a family whose members study together, a seminary whose pupils and teachers reside together, mingling constantly in the familiar and affectionate intercourse of a well-ordered Christian home.

One may still trace, in many customs and arrangements as old as the institution, Miss Lyon's perpetual endeavor to consolidate and to unify. She found daily occasions for gathering all her daughters about her; and thus, as well as in other ways, she brought them close to each other. There were the sacred hours of morning and evening family prayers; the daily assembling for general business; the intentional mingling of members of different classes as room-mates, at table, and frequently—until the senior year—in recitations. And thus to the present time it often comes about that pupils who at first assumed nearly the position of boarders in a hotel, presently find themselves well-beloved daughters in a dear home. If they had come intending to get all they could out of the institution, they, nevertheless, go away eager to do all they can for it.

EXPENSES.

The terms for board and tuition have always been kept as low as possible, while covering the ordinary running expenses. During the first sixteen years the pupils paid only sixty dollars for the forty weeks of the school year, fuel and lights, however, being additional. The terms were afterward gradually raised, but barely enough to meet the increased cost of living. Even as late as 1862 the charge was only eighty dollars a year, but was raised considerably about that time and in years following. From 1867 to 1875 it was one hundred and fifty dollars, not including the cost of warming and lighting, lecture-fees, and one or two other incidental expenses, amounting, in all, to perhaps twenty-five dollars more. At present these items, as well as the board and tuition, are covered by the payment of one hundred and seventy-five dollars. It will be seen that from the first the terms have been about what one would have paid at the given period for board in a country village. Money-making has never been one of the objects contemplated by the institution, though its regular current expenses have generally been kept just within its income. Its teachers, chosen generally from its own graduates, have been so warmly devoted to the seminary, and so fully in sympathy with its benevolent aims, that they preferred its service to the more lucrative positions open to them elsewhere.

THE DOMESTIC DEPARTMENT.

It is well known that the ordinary daily house-work of the family is performed by the young ladies, superintended by the teachers and matrons.* So many erroneous impressions, however, have prevailed in regard to the matter, that it seems necessary to repeat explanations which have often been given before.

Each young lady spends about one hour a day in domestic work. The length of time varies a little, the more laborious or less agreeable tasks being proportionately shorter than the lighter and easier ones. The time occupied varies thus from forty-five to seventy minutes. Only about half an hour's work is done on the Sabbath, while on Wednesday an additional half-hour is necessary. One keeps the position assigned her for a term or more, unless some interference with a recitation or other personal reason makes a change necessary. Pupils are excused from their work whenever their health requires it, the place being temporarily supplied from a reserve corps having no regular appointments.

Various considerations led to the adoption of this system. At Ipswich, as well as in all the schools with which Miss Lyon had been previously connected, the young ladies had boarded in private families. This was inconvenient as well as expensive, and made the institution too dependent upon the neighborhood. The new seminary evidently must board its pupils; and it was decided that the most independent, most economical, and best way of getting the work done would be to arrange matters so that the young ladies could do it for themselves. The decision has never been regretted, nor seriously reconsidered. Miss Lyon had expected this plan to promote the health of her pupils by furnishing them with a little daily exercise of the best kind; their improvement, by preserving and increasing their interest in domestic employments; and their happiness, by relieving them from that depressing dependence on the will of hired domestics to which many a New England household is subject. But as

* A single man-servant is constantly employed for the heavier tasks.

years have passed benefits not clearly foreseen have appeared; certain results are discovered in the discipline of character which could hardly be otherwise secured. One watches the domestic affairs of a family of three hundred going on smoothly and successfully day after day, and year after year, without servants; she can scarcely avoid receiving such an impression as to what system, co-operation, and prompt activity can accomplish as would not easily be gained in any other way. Moreover, she naturally falls into a habit of considering the general good, since she has something to do for all the rest, and every one does something for her. And in the course of time she probably discovers that it is not always pleasanter to be ministered unto than to minister. Were economy the only object, the system might have been dropped, on account of the perplexities it sometimes occasions in arranging recitations. But the seminary could ill afford to dispense with an agency so valuable in training its pupils to bear their part among the workers of the world.*

RELIGIOUS INFLUENCE.

The religious influence of the institution, though unsectarian, has ever been positive and strong. Besides the daily devotional exercises already mentioned, the Bible is regularly studied, and attendance at church is required at least once upon the Sabbath. The pupils perceive that while they are not asked to what denomination they or their friends may belong, it is considered a matter of the deepest consequence whether their lives shall be devoted to selfish aims or con-

* Those interested in studying the subject of education in its relations to health, will find in The Education of American Girls, published by the Putnams of New York, in 1874, an article containing the experience of Mount Holyoke Seminary. It includes statistical tables showing the longevity of graduates from this institution as compared with the graduates of seven of the leading colleges for young men.

secrated to Christ. They are constantly reminded that since they are enjoying privileges provided by Christian benevolence, they are under peculiar obligations to strive to bless others in their turn. They hear much of the various benevolent enterprises of the day, and learn to look forward to an active and useful life. Fully three-fourths of the whole number of students have taught, more or less, after finishing their studies, and many have engaged in missionary work of some kind, either in foreign lands or at home.

Table showing the number of students in Mount Holyoke Seminary in each class annually.

Years.	Junior.	Middle.	Senior.	Years.	Junior.	Junior middle.	Senior middle.	Senior.
1838.....	69	34	4	1862.....	85	70	43	56
1839.....	60	31	12	1863.....	127	87	47	40
1840.....	62	40	17	1864.....	153	98	41	51
1841.....	76	27	10	1865.....	117	87	47	38
1842.....	107	50	15	1866.....	100	87	40	60
1843.....	118	50	16	1867.....	124	59	38	59
1844.....	106	66	34	1868.....	122	64	31	45
1845.....	123	72	51	1869.....	136	64	30	38
1846.....	71	69	42	1870.....	111	84	40	33
1847.....	85	59	44	1871.....	132	77	34	37
1848.....	126	62	47	1872.....	118	74	40	42
1849.....	138	58	23	1873.....	108	75	40	48
1850.....	121	69	34	1874.....	148	74	42	37
1851.....	129	55	60	1875.....	128	95	36	29
1852.....	162	59	31	1876.....	112	77	53	40
1853.....	163	49	46					
1854.....	180	55	43	Whole No. graduates......				1,568
1855.....	162	73	57					
1856.....	156	70	49					
1857.....	139	68	59					
1858.....	147	71	57					
1859.....	150	70	56					
1860.....	148	70	42					
1861.....	157	65	66					

NOTE.—Previous to 1862, the course of study occupied only three years; since that time, four years.

A table showing the attendance at Mount Holyoke Seminary annually from each State and Territory of the Union and from foreign countries.

Years.	United States and Territories.																									
	Alabama.	Arkansas.	California.	Colorado.	Connecticut.	Delaware.	Dist. of Columbia.	Florida.	Georgia.	Illinois.	Indiana.	Indian Territory.	Iowa.	Kansas.	Kentucky.	Louisiana.	Maine.	Maryland.	Massachusetts.	Michigan.	Minnesota.	Missouri.	Mississippi.	Nebraska.	Nevada.	New Hampshire.
1838....	..	..	..	..	13	..	..	..	..	..	..	..	..	..	..	..	..	..	82	..	..	..	..	..	..	3
1839....	..	..	..	..	13	..	..	..	..	..	..	..	..	..	..	..	1	..	64	..	..	1	..	..	..	6
1840....	..	..	..	..	24	..	..	..	..	..	..	..	..	..	..	..	..	..	68	..	..	..	2	..	..	7
1841....	..	..	..	..	18	..	..	..	..	..	..	..	..	..	..	..	..	..	64	..	..	..	1	..	..	11
1842....	..	..	..	..	36	..	1	..	..	..	..	..	..	..	..	..	..	..	87	1	..	..	1	..	..	14
1843....	..	..	..	..	31	..	..	..	2	..	..	..	..	..	1	..	..	..	89	..	..	..	..	..	..	13
1844....	..	..	..	..	41	..	..	..	..	1	..	1	..	..	..	..	..	..	93	..	..	..	..	..	..	11
1845....	1	..	..	..	45	..	..	..	..	1	..	1	..	..	..	..	..	..	109	..	..	..	..	..	..	18
1846....	..	..	..	..	25	..	..	..	..	..	..	1	..	..	..	..	3	..	78	..	..	..	..	..	..	15
1847....	..	..	..	..	32	1	..	..	..	..	..	..	1	..	..	..	3	..	71	..	..	..	..	..	..	14
1848....	..	..	..	..	44	..	..	..	..	2	..	1	1	..	1	..	12	..	79	..	..	1	..	..	..	25
1849....	..	..	..	..	32	..	..	..	..	..	1	2	..	..	1	..	12	1	75	2	..	..	..	..	..	25
1850....	..	..	..	..	33	..	..	..	..	2	..	2	..	..	..	..	7	..	78	3	..	..	..	..	..	20
1851....	..	..	..	..	49	..	..	..	..	6	..	..	..	..	..	..	1	..	73	4	..	..	..	..	..	22
1852....	..	..	..	..	32	..	..	..	1	4	..	1	1	..	..	..	9	..	77	1	..	..	1	..	..	16
1853....	..	..	..	..	45	..	..	..	..	4	..	2	..	..	..	..	5	..	77	..	..	..	1	..	..	22
1854....	..	..	..	..	52	..	1	..	..	9	2	3	..	..	..	..	7	..	68	1	..	1	..	..	..	30
1855....	..	2	..	..	42	1	..	..	..	6	5	..	..	..	..	..	15	..	91	3	..	..	..	..	..	24
1856....	..	..	..	..	42	..	..	..	..	7	3	..	..	1	..	..	21	..	75	..	1	1	..	..	..	25
1857....	1	..	..	..	35	1	..	..	1	5	4	..	1	1	..	..	23	..	75	..	1	..	..	..	..	30
1858....	..	..	..	..	33	..	..	..	1	7	5	..	1	1	..	..	12	..	96	3	..	..	..	..	..	24
1859....	..	..	..	..	39	1	..	..	1	9	1	..	1	1	..	..	14	..	91	2	..	..	..	..	..	22
1860....	..	..	..	..	41	1	..	1	1	7	3	..	2	..	..	..	16	..	77	4	..	1	..	..	..	23
1861....	..	..	..	..	40	..	1	..	..	1	2	..	1	..	1	..	15	..	99	4	..	1	..	..	..	21
1862....	..	..	..	..	32	..	1	..	..	3	3	..	1	..	1	..	10	..	83	4	..	..	1	..	..	19
1863....	..	..	..	..	32	..	2	..	..	5	3	..	..	..	3	..	17	..	101	5	..	1	..	..	..	25
1864....	..	..	..	..	40	..	..	..	..	6	3	..	1	..	2	..	19	..	115	5	..	1	1	..	..	23
1865....	..	..	2	..	44	1	1	..	..	9	..	..	..	..	1	..	11	..	88	5	..	..	..	..	..	16
1866....	..	..	1	..	41	1	..	..	..	4	1	..	1	..	..	..	14	..	85	3	..	..	..	..	..	21
1867....	..	..	3	..	37	..	..	..	..	6	..	..	1	..	..	..	14	..	100	..	1	1	..	..	..	20
1868....	1	..	..	..	32	1	..	..	..	3	..	..	1	..	..	..	22	1	85	..	1	1	..	..	..	23
1869....	..	..	..	..	44	..	..	1	..	1	1	..	3	1	..	..	15	..	90	1	..	..	2	..	..	20
1870....	..	..	..	..	35	1	..	1	..	1	2	..	5	..	..	..	14	..	98	1	..	..	1	1	..	16
1871....	..	..	1	..	43	1	1	1	..	2	1	..	1	1	..	..	13	..	102	..	..	1	..	..	..	18
1872....	..	..	1	1	48	1	1	..	..	1	7	..	..	..	..	..	8	..	87	1	1	1	..	..	..	13
1873....	..	..	..	..	46	1	1	..	..	3	2	..	..	..	..	..	11	..	95	3	1	..	..	..	1	11
1874....	..	..	..	..	54	1	2	..	..	4	2	..	1	1	..	..	9	1	102	4	2	..	..	..	1	14
1875....	..	..	..	..	65	..	2	1	..	3	2	..	1	..	..	..	9	1	101	1	..	..	..	..	..	14
1876....	..	..	..	..	55	..	1	1	1	5	3	..	..	..	1	1	13	2	86	1	2	..	..	..	..	10
Total.	3	2	8	1	1,485	13	15	6	8	127	56	14	25	7	12	1	375	6	3,354	62	10	12	11	1	2	704

A table showing the attendance at Mount Holyoke Seminary annually from each State and Territory, &c.—Continued.

Years	United States and Territories.													Foreign Countries.													Total.
	New Jersey.	New York.	North Carolina.	Ohio.	Pennsylvania.	Rhode Island.	South Carolina.	Tennessee.	Texas.	Vermont.	Virginia.	West Virginia.	Wisconsin.	Canada.	New Brunswick.	Nova Scotia.	Borneo.	China.	Holland.	India.	Italy.	Persia.	Syria.	Sandwich Islands.	Turkey.	West Indies.	
1838..	3	3	..	1	1	3	..	..	..	7	..	..	..	..	..	..	..	..	..	..	..	..	..	..	..	..	116
1839..	2	8	..	..	..	..	..	..	..	8	..	..	..	..	..	..	..	..	..	..	..	..	..	..	..	..	103
1840..	2	3	..	2	..	..	..	..	..	11	..	..	..	..	..	..	..	..	..	..	..	..	..	..	..	..	119
1841..	1	10	..	..	..	..	..	..	..	8	..	..	..	..	..	..	..	..	..	..	..	..	..	..	..	..	113
1842..	6	16	..	1	..	1	..	..	..	6	..	..	1	..	..	..	..	..	..	..	..	..	..	1	..	..	172
1843..	7	29	..	1	..	1	..	..	..	7	1	..	1	1	..	..	..	..	..	..	..	..	..	..	..	..	184
1844..	4	32	..	1	2	..	..	..	..	18	1	..	..	..	..	..	..	..	..	..	..	..	..	1	..	..	206
1845..	3	42	..	4	1	..	..	..	..	19	..	..	..	..	..	..	..	..	..	..	..	..	..	1	1	..	246
1846..	4	39	..	4	1	..	..	..	..	9	..	..	..	2	..	..	..	..	..	..	..	..	..	..	1	..	182
1847..	5	36	..	3	1	..	..	..	..	19	..	..	..	2	..	..	..	..	..	..	..	..	..	..	..	..	188
1848..	6	33	..	4	3	1	..	..	..	16	1	..	1	3	..	1	..	..	..	..	..	..	..	..	..	..	235
1849..	8	34	..	4	4	2	..	..	..	10	1	..	2	1	..	1	..	..	..	..	..	..	..	1	..	..	219
1850..	8	36	..	2	5	1	..	..	..	18	..	..	6	1	..	1	..	..	..	..	..	..	..	1	..	..	224
1851..	8	34	..	6	8	1	..	..	..	24	..	..	5	..	..	..	..	..	..	..	..	..	..	3	..	..	244
1852..	14	44	..	6	7	1	..	..	..	26	2	..	1	1	..	..	..	..	1	..	..	..	..	6	..	..	252
1853..	20	40	1	8	7	2	..	..	..	13	2	..	2	2	..	..	..	..	..	1	..	..	..	4	..	..	258
1854..	16	44	..	9	6	2	..	1	..	20	1	..	2	..	..	..	1	..	..	1	..	..	..	1	..	..	278
1855..	9	53	..	8	8	2	..	1	..	16	..	..	1	..	..	3	..	..	..	2	..	..	..	..	..	..	292
1856..	6	53	..	4	10	3	..	..	..	12	1	..	3	..	..	5	..	..	..	1	..	..	..	..	..	1	275
1857..	13	42	..	3	9	1	..	..	..	11	..	..	1	..	..	5	..	..	..	2	..	..	..	..	..	1	266
1858..	7	40	..	12	11	4	..	..	..	17	..	..	1	..	..	..	..	..	..	..	..	..	..	..	..	..	275
1859..	3	44	..	16	6	3	..	1	1	15	..	..	2	..	..	..	..	..	..	2	..	..	..	..	..	1	276
1860..	4	42	..	8	9	4	..	1	..	13	..	..	1	..	..	1	..	..	..	..	..	..	..	..	..	..	260
1861..	9	48	..	6	6	3	..	..	..	26	..	..	2	..	1	1	..	..	..	..	..	..	..	..	..	..	288
1862..	8	39	..	5	16	2	..	..	..	19	1	..	1	..	1	2	..	..	..	1	..	1	..	..	..	..	254
1863..	14	55	..	3	9	3	..	1	..	11	..	..	3	1	..	3	..	..	..	1	..	2	..	..	1	..	301
1864..	25	56	..	4	10	3	..	1	..	19	..	..	4	..	..	..	..	1	..	2	..	1	..	..	1	..	343
1865..	21	48	..	4	7	2	..	..	..	16	..	1	7	..	..	..	..	1	..	3	..	..	..	..	1	..	289
1866..	15	40	1	11	12	4	..	1	..	15	..	1	9	..	..	..	..	2	..	2	..	..	1	..	1	..	287
1867..	12	30	1	5	11	6	..	..	..	18	..	..	8	1	2	1	..	1	..	..	..	..	1	..	..	..	280
1868..	8	44	..	4	7	1	..	1	..	17	..	..	3	1	2	..	..	1	..	1	..	..	1	..	..	..	262
1869..	12	41	..	5	3	4	..	1	..	16	..	..	2	2	1	..	..	1	..	1	..	..	..	..	..	..	268
1870..	8	35	..	2	10	4	..	..	..	25	..	..	1	1	..	..	..	1	..	4	..	..	..	..	1	..	268
1871..	8	43	..	6	9	4	..	..	..	20	..	..	..	1	..	1	..	..	..	2	..	..	..	..	..	..	280
1872..	13	34	..	2	11	7	..	..	..	29	..	..	1	1	..	..	..	..	..	4	..	..	..	1	..	..	274
1873..	10	36	..	3	5	5	1	..	..	30	..	..	1	1	..	1	..	..	..	..	..	..	..	2	1	..	271
1874..	11	35	..	2	7	5	1	..	..	34	..	..	1	2	..	..	..	..	..	1	1	..	..	2	1	..	301
1875..	12	33	..	4	7	6	..	..	..	21	..	..	1	1	..	..	..	..	..	2	..	..	..	1	..	..	288
1876..	9	36	..	9	10	5	..	1	1	24	1	..	..	1	..	..	..	..	..	2	..	..	..	..	1	..	282
Total	354	1,410	3	182	239	96	2	10	2	663	12	2	74	26	7	26	1	8	1	35	1	4	3	25	10	3	

www.ingramcontent.com/pod-product-compliance
Lightning Source LLC
LaVergne TN
LVHW011144110826
845150LV00008B/2494

* 9 7 8 1 4 1 8 1 9 2 4 3 3 *